HOCKEY
For Kids

Heroes, tips, and facts

Written by
Brian McFarlane

Illustrated by
Bill Slavin

Morrow Junior Books
New York

Acknowledgments

This book is for kids of all ages who love the great game of hockey. Special thanks to former NHL goalie Ken Dryden for his advice and assistance. The professional opinions of fitness expert Al Copetti and nutritionist Fran Berkoff are also much appreciated. Thanks to Valerie Hussey and Ricky Englander of Kids Can Press, and to Laurie Wark, the extremely competent editor, who worked so diligently on the project.

Text copyright © 1996 by Brian McFarlane
Illustrations copyright © 1994 by Bill Slavin
First published in Canada in 1994 by Kids Can Press,
29 Birch Avenue, Toronto, Ontario, Canada M4V 1E2

Library of Congress Cataloging-in-Publication Data
McFarlane, Brian.
Hockey for kids: heroes, tips, and facts / written by Brian McFarlane: illustrated by Bill Slavin. p. cm.
"First published in Canada in 1994 by Kids Can Press"—T.p. verso.
Includes index.
Summary: Surveys the sport of hockey, covering its history, equipment, techniques, players, and more.
ISBN 0-688-15026-8
1. Hockey—Juvenile literature. [1. Hockey.] I. Slavin, Bill, ill. II. Title. GV847.25.M34 1996 796.962—dc20 96-12618 CIP AC

Photo credits
All photos Bruce Bennett Studios except:
Canada Wide Feature Photos: 41 (bottom). City of Toronto archives, James 475: 41 (top). Hockey Hall of Fame Archives: 54 (bottom left), 56 (right). Household/Hockey Hall of Fame: 61 (top). Imperial Oil-Turofsky/Hockey Hall of Fame: 54 (top right, bottom right), 57 (top left), 58 (bottom left). Doug MacLellan/Hockey Hall of Fame: 46 (top), 63 (sidebar: middle right, bottom right). Brian McFarlane Collection: 63 (sidebar: top right, bottom left). VB/Hockey Hall of Fame: 60, 61 (bottom).

CONTENTS

Chapter 1

Drop the puck

Let's play hockey — 4
Who invented hockey? — 8
The puck stops here — 10
That's a penalty — 12
Icing and offside — 14
Hockey talk — 16

Chapter 2

Get playing

Equipment know-how — 18
If the skate fits — 20
Warm it up — 22
Get skating! — 24
The scoop on sticks — 26
What coaches look for — 28
Scoring goals — 30
He shoots! He scores! — 32

Chapter 3

The pros

The road to the pros — 34
Game day — 36
Wear number 13? Not me! — 38
Women in hockey — 40
Meet a referee — 44
The Stanley Cup — 46
Stanley Cup adventures — 48

Chapter 4

Stars of the game

Hockey heroes — 50
Goal guardians — 54
Great moments in hockey — 56
And the winner is... — 58
The Hockey Hall of Fame — 60
Make a hockey scrapbook — 62
Index — 64

CHAPTER 1

Drop the puck

Let's play hockey

You likely already know that the aim in hockey is to put the puck in the opposing team's net — as often as possible. At the same time, you try to keep your opponents from putting the puck in your net. These basic principles, called offensive and defensive team play, may seem confusing at first, but read on.

The ice

A National Hockey League (NHL) hockey arena or "rink" is approximately 200 feet long and 85 feet wide. The boards surrounding the rink are topped with shatterproof glass that protects the spectators from flying pucks and sticks.

Five lines are painted on the ice. The goal nets sit on the goal lines, which are painted 11 feet out from the end boards. The two blue lines divide the rink into three different zones called defensive, offensive, and neutral zones. Both ends of the rink can be known as offensive and defensive, depending on the point of view of each team. The end your own goal net is in is known as your defensive zone and the opposite end is your offensive zone. The center-ice red line divides the rink in half. The purpose of the lines is to keep the players on the move and to prevent some of them from standing around in front of the opposing net waiting for a pass.

There are five large circles painted on the ice. These are used for facing off the puck. During a face-off, only the two players facing off are allowed within the circle.

Players and playing

The game is divided into three 20-minute periods in the NHL. If the score is tied at the end of the 60 minutes of play, there is a five-minute overtime period, which ends when the first overtime goal is scored. If no one scores in the five minutes, the game ends in a tie.

A professional team consists of up to 20 players. Big-league teams generally carry as many as twelve forwards, six defensemen, and two goaltenders, as

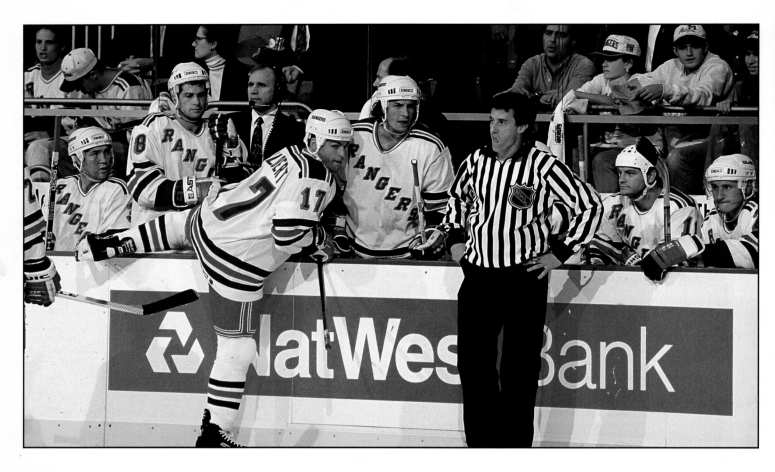

well as a coach and his assistants, a manager and his assistants, and trainers, equipment managers, and team doctors.

Three forwards play together on a line (left wing, right wing, and center). The center tries to win face-offs, and they all work to set up plays for each other. Forwards must be fast skaters and hard shooters. They try to move the puck — by skating with it, by stickhandling it, or by passing it back and forth — into the other team's defensive zone. Their destination is the "slot" (an area directly in front of the goalie). They know most goals are scored from the slot. From that position, they'll try to beat the goalie with a hard shot — such as a wrist shot, a slap shot, or a backhander — aimed at the corners of the net. Sometimes they try to "deke" the goalie — by faking him out of position — in an attempt to score.

What's the other team doing while this is going on? It is playing defensive hockey. The two defensemen, whose job it is to prevent opponents from scoring, are checking hard in the slot — stickchecking and bodychecking. The defensive team's forwards have come back and they are checking, too. The goalie, crouched over, will

sometimes move out of his net, to "cut down the angles" to the goal, making it very difficult for the attacking team to score.

The puck changes hands frequently, often several times each minute. If players on the defending team come up with the puck deep in their own zone, they have a break-out play planned — one that gets the puck quickly out of their zone. When that happens, the players on the opposing team rush back toward their zone and play defensive hockey. This is called backchecking.

If players in control of the puck can't organize a break-out play from their own zone, it's often because the opposing team sends in speedy forwards to pressure them. This is called forechecking.

Hockey is so fast that players tire quickly. Remember, they skate in short bursts at speeds up to 30 miles per hour, so they can stay on the ice for only a minute or two. Hockey players often change lines "on the fly" by jumping from the bench to the ice while teammates are jumping from the ice to the bench. In no other sport are players allowed to substitute for others without a break in the action.

Who invented hockey?

Many hundreds of years ago, a boy named Hans lived in a small village in northern Europe. There weren't many roads where Hans lived, but there were lots of waterways. In winter, Hans and his friends traveled along the frozen rivers from one place to another on handmade skis, snowshoes, or skates.

One day, Hans was skating along on his new skates, which had handmade bone blades on them. He picked up a tree branch and carried it with him because he found the branch helped him keep his balance as he skated along. Then, ahead of him, Hans noticed a small stone on the ice. He struck the stone with his branch and sent it skimming over the smooth surface. Hey, that was fun!

Then Hans came upon a group of his friends. Soon, they all had branches and were pushing stones across the ice. They began to play with just one stone and tried to get it away from each other.

Was this the first game of hockey? It could have been — it resembled a game known as shinny, which is a crude form of hockey. We

don't really know who the first hockey players were or where they lived. We do know skating was a favorite winter pastime in Holland centuries ago. Even the word skate is said to come from the Dutch word *schaat*.

Eventually, iron skate blades replaced the bone or wooden blades. Short sticks, almost like golf clubs, appeared, and the disk or ball the players batted over the ice became known as a puck.

It's possible, of course, that other kids might have discovered the fun of playing on ice with a stick and a stone long before Hans did. They may have lived in Finland, Norway, Sweden, Scotland, or England, for skating has a long history in those countries as well. Wherever

hockey started, it wasn't long before people caught on to this exciting winter sport. By 1800, many people from northern Europe and the British Isles had settled in Canada. They brought their skates with them, and skating quickly became everybody's favorite winter sport.

Soon these pioneers devised a team game similar to the games of shinny played today. The players set up two goals marked with stones or blocks of wood, and players used sticks cut from tree branches. Others used field-hockey sticks brought from England. The puck was either a ball, a piece of bone, or a chunk of wood.

Perhaps the players got the idea for their new game from watching Native Americans play

lacrosse. Perhaps the new settlers brought the idea with them, possibly from field hockey, when they came to Canada. This new game was fast, it was fun, and someone, at some time, began to call it hockey.

Three Canadian cities — Halifax, Kingston, and Montreal — claim credit for introducing ice hockey. But the first official hockey game, with written rules, was probably played in 1875 at McGill University in Montreal. These "McGill rules" are the basis for the rules used today.

Hockey soon became so popular across Canada that a governor general, Lord Stanley of Preston, decided to donate a small silver bowl in 1893 to the top team. That trophy became known as the Stanley Cup.

The puck stops here

Footballs, baseballs, basketballs, soccer balls, tennis balls, and pucks — one of these things is not like the others. Hockey is one of the few sports that doesn't use a ball — and it's the only sport that uses a puck.

Legend has it the puck was invented one night in the 1800s during a game of shinny. In those days, the players used a hard rubber ball to play, and it frequently flew over the boards and bounced all around the arena. On this night, the bouncing ball crashed through an expensive window, and the arena manager grabbed the ball and pared off two sections of it with his jackknife. He threw the flat center portion back on the ice, and the game continued with the newly shaped object. Because the puck slid along the ice instead of bouncing, it was easier to control and the game became more fun to play, not to mention less dangerous to watch.

Some NHL teams use up to 5000 pucks in a season.

At the 1996 All-Star game, the NHL and Fox Sports unveiled the FoxTrax system for highlighting the puck. TV viewers saw a glow around the puck when it was carried or passed. On fast shots, a red comet tail trailed the puck. The puck had a circuit board inside and infrared emitters on the outside.

10

How pucks are made

Millions of pucks are made every year. Huge batches of rubber — enough to make a thousand pucks — are mixed with coal dust. The mixture is put in machines that churn out a roll of rubber like a huge sausage. A heavy slicer cuts the rubber into 6-ounce pucks (called blanks at this stage), which are placed in molds.

Each mold can hold 27 blanks. From then on it's a lot like making muffins. Team emblems or logos are glued on the blanks, and the molds are cooked for 20 minutes. To make sure the pucks are shaped perfectly, they're pressed (while cooking) under 2000 pounds of pressure. After that, they are packaged and shipped and ready for NHL stars to take their best shot at them.

A bout 30 to 40 pucks are used in most big-league games.

Hockey leagues have experimented with pucks of different sizes and colors. But they always come back to the black vulcanized rubber pucks that hold their shape and chip less frequently than colored pucks.

During a playoff game that took place when pro hockey was still played on natural ice, the puck fell through the ice and could not be recovered.

Back in the early 1900s, if the puck was shot out among the spectators, the fan who caught it was expected to throw it back on the ice. But during the 1902 playoffs, a Winnipeg fan caught the puck — and kept it! That started a tradition still followed today.

Pucks are placed in a freezer before big-league games. Frozen pucks slide better and bounce less than nonfrozen pucks.

In a 1902 playoff game between Toronto and Winnipeg, the puck split in half. "Chummy" Hill of Toronto shot one half past the Winnipeg goalie, and the referee counted it as a goal!

That's a penalty

Referees hand out penalties to keep the game moving and to protect the players from being hurt. If you play hockey, you should avoid getting penalties because you put your team at a disadvantage — your teammates must play without you while you're in the penalty box.

Here are some of the types of hockey penalties.

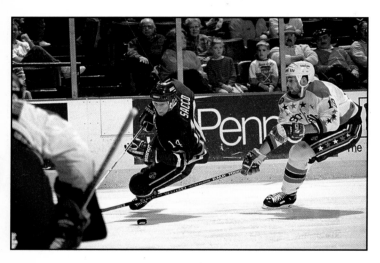

Minor penalty

When you are given a minor penalty, you must sit in the penalty box for two minutes while your team plays shorthanded. If, however, the opposing team scores a goal while you are in the box, you may immediately return to the ice. Minor penalties are handed out for fouls such as tripping, slashing, holding, and elbowing.

Major penalty

If you are caught bodychecking, cross-checking, elbowing, charging, or tripping in such a manner that causes an opponent to be thrown violently into the boards, you are given a major penalty and must sit in the penalty box for five minutes. You must not leave the box until the full five minutes have been served, even if the opposing team scores. In the NHL, when you get a major penalty for causing an injury to a player's face or head with your stick, you must pay a $100 fine.

Misconduct penalty

Using abusive language, banging the boards with your stick, deliberately throwing equipment out of the playing area, or refusing to obey the referee will get you a misconduct penalty. If you are charged with a misconduct penalty you must leave the game for ten minutes, but your team is allowed to substitute for you during that time. In the NHL, a misconduct penalty also brings a fine of $100.

Game misconduct

If you're charged with a game misconduct penalty, you are suspended for the rest of that game and, in the NHL, fined $200. However, your team may put a substitute on the ice immediately. A game misconduct is automatically given to a player who gets involved in a fight between two other players. It can also be given to a player who has earned a misconduct penalty and continues to behave in the manner that earned him the misconduct penalty in the first place.

Match penalty

A match penalty is a penalty given to any player who deliberately attempts to injure another player. You must leave the ice immediately if you receive one. A substitute player may replace you after five minutes of playing time. In the NHL, the referee also reports your match penalty to the commissioner for possible further discipline.

Gross misconduct penalty

It seldom happens, but a referee may impose a gross misconduct penalty on a player, manager, or coach, possibly for getting involved physically with the spectators. If you get a gross misconduct penalty in the NHL, you are suspended for the rest of the game, fined $200, and your case is referred to the commissioner for further disciplinary action.

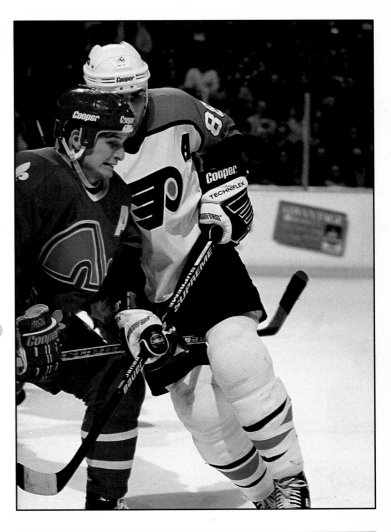

Did you know?

On March 31, 1991, Chris Nilan of the Boston Bruins set an NHL record when he received ten penalties in a single game. In a game against Hartford, Nilan received six minors, two majors, one ten-minute misconduct, and one game misconduct.

Icing and offside

Do you find some of the most puzzling rules in hockey are those that govern icing the puck and playing offside? You'll be an expert on both subjects after you read these explanations.

Icing the puck

Players who shoot the puck from their own side of the center-ice line to a point behind the opposing team's goal line are penalized for "icing the puck." When an opposing player touches the "iced" puck, a linesman blows the whistle and the puck is brought back to be faced off near the net of the team that iced the puck. If there was no rule against "icing the puck," a team being outplayed might shoot the puck down the ice at every opportunity. That would be a boring game to watch and play, wouldn't it?

Icing the puck is not called if:
- the goalie plays the puck by leaving his net
- the team shooting it is playing shorthanded
- one of the opponents is able to reach the puck (in the opinion of the linesman) before it crosses the goal line, but chooses not to in the hope of getting an icing call

Icing is not called if the goalie plays the puck by leaving his net.

Offside

The purpose of the offside rule is to prevent one team from sending a player deep into the opposing team's zone to wait for a long pass and gain an unfair advantage.

A player is offside when:

- the puck crosses her opponent's blue line after she does
- she takes a pass that started behind her own blue line, when she is beyond the center-ice line

An offside by the attacking team. The pass receiver's skates are over the blue line.

An offside from the defensive zone. The puck crosses two lines to a receiver.

Hockey talk

Can you figure out what this hockey announcer is saying?

"Steve Yzerman, after winning the draw and deking a defenseman, scored with a backhand drive from the slot. It was upstairs on the power play to complete his hat trick."

Do you understand what the announcer said? Sometimes it seems as if hockey has its own language! Here's the translation: Steve won the face-off, faked his way past a defenseman, and scored his third goal of the game with a high backhand shot from in front of the opposing team's goal while his team held a man advantage because of a penalty.

Here are some more translations of hockey talk.

Breakaway: When the puck carrier has just one defender — the goalie — to beat.

Checking: Using your body or stick to block or interfere with an opponent. It's legal when an opponent has the puck or was the last player to touch it.

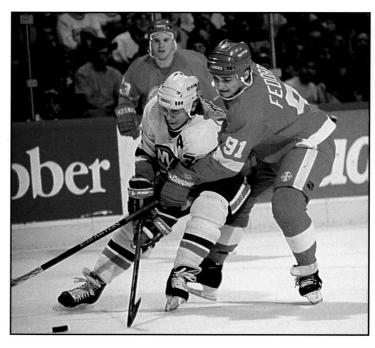

Farm team: The minor league affiliate of an NHL team.

Getting a hat trick: You already know this means scoring three goals in a game. A "pure" hat trick is three consecutive goals by the same player in a game. The expression comes from the fact that years ago, in some sports, a three-goal performer was often presented with a bowler hat.

Splitting the defense: When a player with the puck dashes between two opposing defensemen.

Head-manning the puck: This is the technique of passing the puck quickly ahead to a teammate farthest up the ice, making him the head man of the attacking unit.

Ragging the puck: If a player is ragging the puck he's controlling it for several seconds through clever skating and stickhandling. A player may do this to kill off penalty time or to protect a lead late in the game.

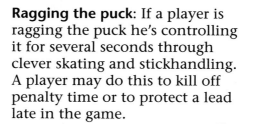

Point man: A player on the attacking team (usually a defenseman) who takes up a position just inside the opposing team's blue line. This helps to keep the puck in the opposing team's zone and sets the point man up for a shot on goal.

Shutout: When one team stops the other team from scoring for the full 60 minutes of a game. The winning team's goalie is credited with a shutout in the goaltending statistics.

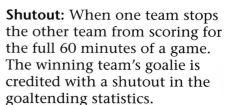

Playing shorthanded: When a penalty is given to a player, a substitute is not allowed to take her place on the ice. Her team plays shorthanded until she is released from the penalty box.

Freezing the puck: Putting the puck in the freezer? Actually, it can mean that. Since cold pucks slide on ice better than pucks kept at room temperature, pucks are frozen before each game. But during a game, freezing the puck means pinning it against the boards or net with your stick if you're being checked. Deliberately freezing the puck, or doing it when you're not being checked, can lead to a penalty.

CHAPTER 2

Get playing

Equipment know-how

Smart hockey players know they're less likely to be injured if they're in good physical condition, play by the rules, and protect their bodies with the right equipment. You'll play better and with more confidence if you're properly outfitted. Here are some pointers to keep in mind when you're choosing equipment.

Did you know?

Hockey was the first team sport to place numbers on the backs of uniforms. It's said the idea came from Joe Patrick, an organizer of the Pacific Coast Hockey League, in 1911. He saw a photograph in a newspaper from England showing a cross-country runner wearing a number pinned to his back. Joe thought it was a good idea that should be tried in hockey. His two sons,who ran the Vancouver and Victoria teams, agreed. On opening night of the 1911–12 season, all players in the league wore numbers, and within three years, numbered jerseys were adopted by teams in all leagues.

Jersey and stockings

They should be light, well-ventilated to prevent heat buildup, resistant to constant abrasion, and comfortable. The best stockings have no feet, just a loop that circles the arch of your foot.

Athletic supporter and cup

The supporter, or jockstrap, should have a durable elastic waistband. The cup should be of high-impact polyethylene with foam-cushion edges. Girls should wear a similar protector called a jillstrap.

Garter belt

Elasticized for comfort, your garter belt should have four stocking holders.

Skates

You won't get very far without skates, probably the most important part of your equipment. Last year's skates should be tested before each season to find out if they still fit comfortably. Never buy new skates without lacing them up at least once. When a skate is laced, your foot is held at the back of the boot, giving you an exact idea of the boot's comfort and size. Have your skates sharpened only when necessary, and have a qualified person do it. (For more on skates, see page 20.)

Shoulder pads

Avoid cumbersome, bulky pads that restrict the natural motion of your arms and shoulders. The new models provide maximum protection for the shoulders, collarbone, biceps, ribs, and spine. Female players should wear shoulder pads with a long front to protect the chest area.

Elbow pads

Look for quality elbow pads that are preshaped to the contour of your elbow. Elbow pads that are too big will slip away from your elbows, and you could get injured.

Helmet and mask

Never participate in a game or practice without a helmet and mask to protect your head and face. It's a fact that helmets and masks prevent head and eye injuries. Take time to select a helmet that will give you maximum protection and comfort.

Shin guards

Shin guards don't have to be expensive to provide adequate protection, but it is important to find the proper length of pad. Make sure the kneecap protector fits squarely over your knee. The bottom of the guard should stop at the top of the skate boot. Look for shin guards with wraparound knee and shin flares for complete protection.

Gloves

Select gloves carefully. You must protect your hands without sacrificing control of your stick. Make certain the thumb area is well protected. When you're testing out gloves, handle a stick while wearing them to get an idea of the stick control they allow.

Hockey pants

If you are of average build, your hockey pants should be much larger than your waist size. Look for lightweight pants that provide full protection and comfort. Hold your pants in position with a set of adjustable suspenders.

Hockey stick

When you select a hockey stick, it's important to get the proper lie (the angle between the blade and the shaft) and the proper length. Sawing a bit off a too-long shaft can make a world of difference in controlling the puck.

(For more on sticks, see page 26.)

If the skate fits

If you wiggle your toes in your street shoes, chances are your toes don't reach right up to the front of the shoes. But when you slip your foot into a hockey boot, it's important your toes are right up front. When they are, and you dig in on the ice, you'll get much better leverage. That's why hockey boots are wide in front. And that's why your skates should be a size smaller than your shoes. When you wear a skate that fits snugly, with excellent support in the heel of the boot, you'll skate better without tiring. Follow the pointers on these pages when you're looking for skates.

Take care of your skates. Wipe moisture off them after games and practices. When you take your skates off, unlace them more than halfway down and pull the tongue out, letting air get inside the skate to dry it out. Perspiration from your feet contains body salts that will eat into the skate and eventually damage the lining.

Sergei Fedorov is one of the NHL's fastest skaters.

Not only is Paul Kariya a speedy skater, he's also known for his stickhandling and playmaking.

The ice flies as Peter Bondra eludes a checker.

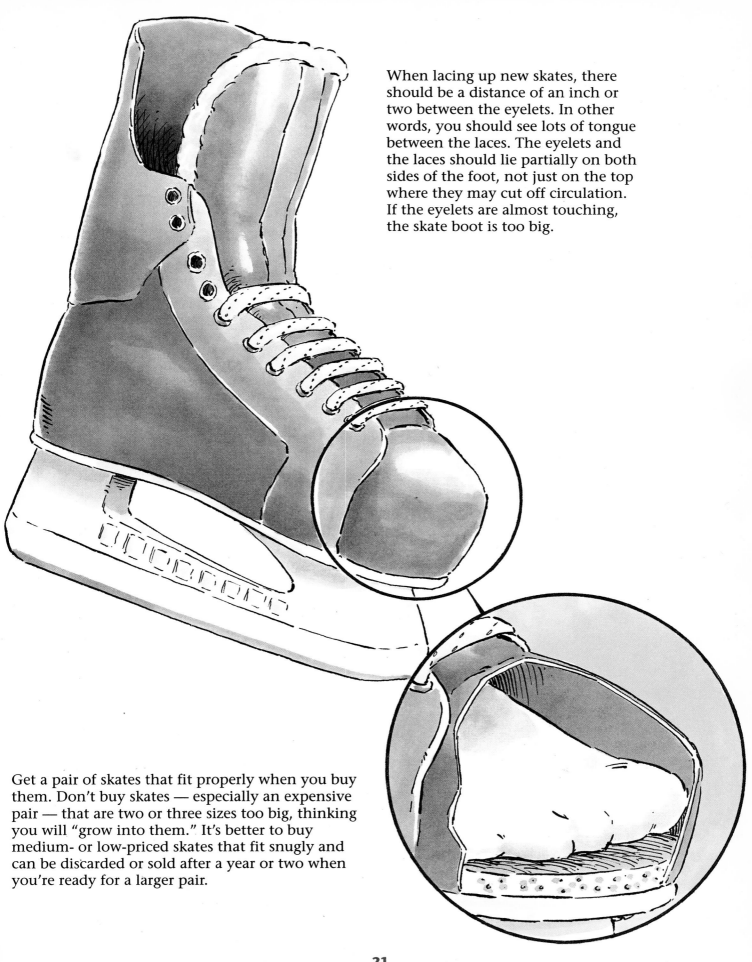

When lacing up new skates, there should be a distance of an inch or two between the eyelets. In other words, you should see lots of tongue between the laces. The eyelets and the laces should lie partially on both sides of the foot, not just on the top where they may cut off circulation. If the eyelets are almost touching, the skate boot is too big.

Get a pair of skates that fit properly when you buy them. Don't buy skates — especially an expensive pair — that are two or three sizes too big, thinking you will "grow into them." It's better to buy medium- or low-priced skates that fit snugly and can be discarded or sold after a year or two when you're ready for a larger pair.

Warm it up

When you see hockey players skating around before a game, they're not just checking out the competition — they're warming up. You need to be warmed up for a game or practice to prepare your muscles for the fast skating, as well as the bumps and falls and shots you'll be taking. Warm-up exercises and stretches not only loosen you up, they help you avoid injuries such as muscle pulls or strains. So before you get on the ice, take some time to stretch your muscles, and remember to hold each stretch for at least 15 seconds, extending only as far as you feel comfortable. Here are some warm-up exercises to try once you hit the ice. Remember, you should do warm-ups slowly and repeat them several times.

Kicking the stick

With your hockey stick held in front of you at about shoulder height, lift your right skate to touch the stick while balancing on your left skate. Then repeat the exercise, this time lifting your left skate and balancing on your right. Do this warm-up exercise slowly and carefully. As it becomes easier, lift the stick higher, making it a more difficult target to reach. You'll be warming up your hamstring, groin, and front thigh muscles.

Stretch the groin

After skating around the ice a few times to loosen up, try gliding along on one skate with the gliding knee bent. Extend the other leg behind you with the foot turned so your skate blade is flat on the ice. Keep your head up and hold your stick in the same hand as your gliding foot. Use your stick for balance and try to keep most of your weight on the ball of your gliding foot. Now try the same exercise, reversing the position of your feet. This exercise will help prevent groin pulls, a common complaint with hockey players.

Hamming it up

Glide along on your skates and hold your stick over your head. Then bend over and touch your toes with your stick, keeping your legs slightly bent. You'll feel the stretch in your hamstring muscles, the long muscles in the backs of your legs. Don't lean forward as you bend, or you may fall over.

Hands up for this groin exercise

Skate slowly, feet shoulder-width apart, with your hockey stick held in both hands over your head. Spread your legs apart as far as is comfortably possible. Then bend over from the waist, bringing your hockey stick down to your skates. Hold it there. Now bring it back to its original position over your head as you quickly move your feet back to a normal position.

Get skating!

If you want to become a good hockey player, skating is the first and most important skill to master. As you improve, you'll soon develop your own style of skating, but there are a few fundamentals essential to becoming a good skater. Skate with your knees bent and your head up. Lean forward to keep your weight in front of you, and learn to make quick stops and turns. Develop strong leg and hip action, and practice skating forward and backward as fast as you can. The better you get, the more fun you'll have playing hockey. Try some of the games on these pages to practice your skating skills.

Hawks and hares

Here's a great game to play with your friends or teammates. It develops speed and agility and is played without using sticks or pucks.

All the skaters (the Hares) but one line up behind the two blue lines, half of them behind each line. The extra player (the Hawk) stands at center ice. When he shouts "Hawk," all the players must cross to the opposite blue line, trying not to be touched by the Hawk. A skater who is touched by the Hawk also becomes a Hawk and helps to catch the others. The last Hare to be touched is the winner.

You're it!

Here's another fast-moving game for ten to twenty players that can be played at one end of a hockey rink — inside the blue line.

All players but one have a puck. The player without a puck is "It." "It" chases the other players and gets a puck away from one of them. "It" must stickhandle the puck into the goal crease and put the puck in the net. The player who lost the puck tries to steal it back before it enters the crease. If she fails, she joins "It" in another chase for more pucks. The last player with a puck is the winner.

Heavy traffic

Here's a game that calls for some fancy stickhandling. It can be played on one-third of a hockey rink, using the two face-off circles and the ice in between them.

The two teams consist of five to ten players each, and each player has a stick and a puck. Each team gathers within its circle and the players stickhandle around without leaving the circle. On a signal, the teams switch circles. Watch out for all those players coming in the opposite direction! The winning team is the one that gets all its players into the other circle first. Each player must be in a stationary hockey stance with a puck on his stick in front of him for the round to be complete. Make it a four-out-of-seven series — just like the Stanley Cup finals.

He shoots, he scores — backward?

Fred "Cyclone" Taylor, playing for Renfrew, Ontario, boasted in 1910 that he could score a goal while skating backward. In the last game of the regular season, Renfrew blasted Ottawa 17–2. It was in this game that Taylor rushed in on goal, turned around, and with his back to the Ottawa goalie, ripped a hard shot to score in the corner of the net.

The scoop on sticks

Canada's pioneer players made sticks from tree branches, especially ash. These primitive sticks, patterned after field-hockey sticks, were short and heavy, with blades that curved up. Players had to skate crouched over to use them. Finally, someone decided to make lighter sticks with wide blades and longer shafts so players could skate more easily and shoot the puck harder.

Two-piece sticks (with the blade fitted and glued into the shaft)

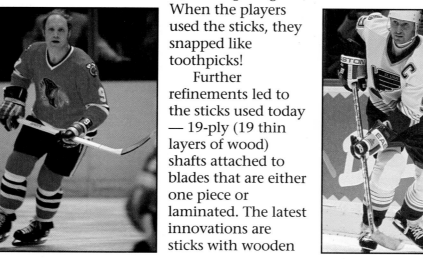

appeared in the early 1930s and soon replaced the old one-piece models. In the 1970s, laminated sticks (layers of thin strips of wood glued together to form shaft and blade) were introduced. However, the first of these sticks were not all successful. One shipment froze in a boxcar, making the glue brittle. When the players used the sticks, they snapped like toothpicks!

Further refinements led to the sticks used today — 19-ply (19 thin layers of wood) shafts attached to blades that are either one piece or laminated. The latest innovations are sticks with wooden cores reinforced by fiberglass, sticks with aluminum shafts and replacement blades, and the totally synthetic stick.

Aluminum sticks are becoming more and more popular in the NHL. Wayne Gretzky, Brett Hull, and Jeremy Roenick are some of the many players who use them. They are expensive, but the shaft lasts for several months and a broken blade can easily be replaced. Some NHL players replace 18 to 24 blades a month.

Selecting a stick

Wayne Gretzky uses a stick that is light and stiff and has a moderate curve in the blade. He is most concerned about the lie (the angle between the blade and the shaft) of the stick and the stiffness of the shaft. Tall players, such as Mario Lemieux, are more concerned about the length of the stick. Mario uses a 60-inch shaft — the maximum length allowed — and averages one stick per period. Finding a stick you're comfortable with is very important. Here are some tips to help you make your decision.

- Select a stick that suits your stance on the ice. Forget about selecting a stick that comes up to your chin or nose. Decide about stick length when you are on the ice — in your skates. Get a comfortable grip on the stick and then decide on length.

- Experiment with sticks — borrow a teammate's stick for a few minutes. If it has a shorter shaft or a different curve in the blade, you might find it suits you better than your own. Try different methods of taping a knob on the end of the stick for a better grip.

How to tape a stick

You'll find taping the blade of your stick leads to better puck control. It also helps keep the blade dry. Begin taping at the heel of the blade and work your way to the end of the blade. One layer of tape is enough.

The upper shaft of the stick should be taped so it can be gripped more firmly. Some players use black tape on the shaft, building up to a little knob. Then they cover the black tape with white tape to protect their gloves from the stickiness of the black tape.

To make a knob at the end of your stick, unroll about 18 inches of hockey tape. Attach the end of the tape to

the end of your stick and let the roll dangle down so that it turns and sticks to itself (you'll have to spin the roll a little). Attach this bumpy tape to the end of your stick and repeat until you have a knob that is about the size you want. Carefully wrap more tape over the knob until it is smooth and even all around.

What coaches look for

Do you ever wonder what your coach sees in you? Does he think you're a smart player with the puck? Why does he play you on defense instead of on one of the forward lines? What does a coach look for in a player anyway?

No matter what the level of hockey — Pee Wee to pro — coaches look for disciplined players and players with lots of skills. All coaches rate skating as an important skill. Without good skaters, a team is not likely to be successful. Shooting, passing, checking, and stickhandling skills are also important if you hope to play junior, college, or professional hockey. Good coaches can teach these skills, but it's up to you to master them. If you play hockey, you may have many coaches over the years. Each one will be different and will have his or her own coaching style and philosophy. Try to learn as much as you can from all of your coaches.

Most coaches have some sort of plan in organizing a team. A good coach will try to place the players in the positions on the ice that suit them best, and he will have definite ideas of how the team should forecheck, backcheck, and kill penalties. One skill coaches often look for in a player is checking. Many players are strong offensively — they can shoot and score goals — but they have never concentrated on checking. The success of a team will often depend on capable checking, so the sooner you learn the skills of checking the better.

Bodychecking

To be a good checker, it is not necessary to hand out bruising bodychecks. It's often enough to stay close to the player you're checking, to bump him slightly with your body and knock the puck away with your stick. It's important to learn how to check without drawing penalties.

The sweep check

The sweep check is an attempt to sweep the puck away from your opponent. It is done with a sweeping motion of the stick held in one hand. It is a well-timed slap at the puck to jar it loose from your opponent's stick.

The poke check

The poke check, like the sweep check, is used to knock the puck away from your opponent. It is a quick, one-handed thrust forward, aimed at the puck or stick blade of your opponent. Defensemen find the poke check particularly useful.

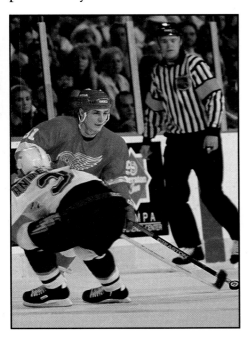

The stick lift

Simply catch up to the puck carrier and lift her stick by placing your stick under hers and raising it. Once her stick is raised, try to scoop the puck away from her.

Forechecking

If you go into the offensive zone after an opposing player who has the puck, you're forechecking. Only one attacking player forechecks while a linemate gets ready to pick up the loose puck. The most important thing in forechecking is to take the puck carrier out of the play. Try to force him close to the boards by skating toward him at an angle. If you skate straight at him, he can move either to his left or his right.

Backchecking

You must learn to come back when the other team is on the attack. Stay between your opponent and the puck. If he gets the puck, try one of the stick checks or use your body to take him out of the play. When possible, rub him along the boards with a shoulder check, forcing him to give up the puck.

Scoring goals

"You can't score if you don't shoot the puck."

How often have you heard that from your coach? Shooting is something you should practice whenever you get a chance. Most pros shoot the puck well because they work on their shot at every opportunity. When they were young, they may have shot a ball against a garage door, or fired away at a board or canvas target set up in the backyard. Here are some drills you can try to help you score more often. With practice, you'll turn your close calls into sure things and make that red goal light flash.

Watch the goalie

If the goalie stands back in her net, common sense tells a forward to shoot for the openings. If the goalie moves out in front of the crease, she cuts down the angles to the net, making it more difficult to score. A shooter moving in on the goalie will find her easier to deke if she's well out of her net, so keep an eye on what the goalie's doing.

Screening a shot

In a game or practice, the goalie often can't see the shooter because other players have skated in front of the net, screening the shot. Practice shooting through a screen; it often pays off in a goal.

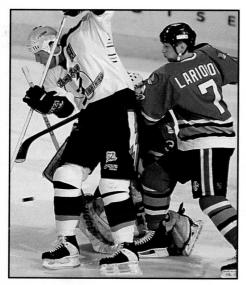

Sometimes a goalie is so screened on a shot that he's almost impossible to see.

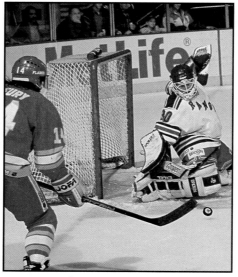

Often a great save will result in a rebound that a player can pounce on.

If the goalie is well out of his net, try deking to get the puck past him.

Tip the puck in

Stand off to the side of the net and pass the puck back to your defenseman. When he shoots at the net, use the blade of your stick to change the direction of the shot, tipping the puck past the goalie. Try to deflect the puck to the corners of the net and through the goalie's legs.

Passing, shooting, and scoring

Stand in front of the goalie and have a teammate send you good, hard passes. If possible, shoot the puck without stopping it first. Aim for the corners of the net. Occasionally try to shoot the puck between the goalie's legs.

Scoring a goal is hard work, but what a great feeling!

Off-ice shooting

You can practice shooting when you're not on the ice by making your own hockey target board. Paint circles on your board or get an adult to help you cut four corner holes in a piece of plywood, and set it up against a wall or backyard fence. Use a piece of Masonite or some other smooth surface as a platform from which to shoot the puck. Now see how often you can hit the targets. Try moving the board farther away or closer to you. Challenge your friends to a shoot-out and see who can score the most goals.

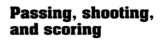

He shoots! He scores!

Hi, hockey fans! Welcome to our intermission show. Tonight on "Brian Talks Hockey," we're going to talk about what it takes to score goals. We've got an expert here with us tonight, Brett Hull.

Brian: Brett, you've scored a lot of goals with your shot. What makes you such a good shooter?

Brett: You know what they say, Brian — practice makes perfect. I love to shoot the puck, so practicing my shots is never a chore. It's fun.

Brian: Brett, can you explain how you shoot the puck?

Brett: If I'm carrying the puck in on goal, I cradle it with my stick — with the puck somewhere in the center of the blade. I can feel it in my hands when the puck is in the right spot. With my head up, I can see the mesh in behind the goalie. That's what I want to hit: the place where the goalie's not. With a sweeping motion, and using lots of wrist and arm action, I shoot for an opening. I'm a right-handed shooter, so most of the power for the shot comes from my right leg.

Brian: What's the position of your hands when you're shooting?

Brett: Before I shoot, I shift my hands to a position most comfortable to me. Not too far apart or I won't get enough flexibility or whip in the stick. Not too close together or I won't get enough power from my lower hand. Like most players, I've learned the best hand positions for me through trial and error.

Brian: What about following through on your shot?

Brett: Follow-through is very important. Good shooters get hard, accurate shots when they follow through until the stick blade is pointing toward the target.

Brian: Do you use a different technique on slap shots?

Brett: It's pretty much the same, with a couple of exceptions. When you pull your stick back for a slap shot, you must know where the puck is on the ice. Take a quick look down as you wind up for the shot, so you'll know where to make contact.

Also, grip the shaft of the stick a little tighter, because you don't want the blade to turn in your hands when you strike the ice and the puck. When I release a slap shot, I get my full weight into it.

Brian: How much time do you take to get your shot away?

Brett: Not much. Sometimes just a split second, especially when I'm in the slot and there's an

opposing player coming at me. That's when I rely on strong wrist and shoulder action because there's no time to throw my full weight into the shot.

Brian: Thanks for those great tips, Brett. I'm sure all the young players watching tonight will try them out. That's our show for tonight. In a moment, the play-by-play of the second period.

33

CHAPTER 3

The pros

The road to the pros

Have you ever dreamed of being a professional hockey player? Lots of kids have that dream, but the road that takes you from your first team to a professional hockey team can be a long one — with many obstacles along the way. Only the most determined and the most skillful players press on to the pros.

After traveling the road that leads to the pros for a number of years, many players drop out for various reasons. Some players decide pro hockey just isn't for them, and they pursue other careers. Many players are aware they lack the skills to become NHL players, and they may get involved in other sports. Others become more involved in school or hobbies, and some have simply had their fill of organized hockey after ten or twelve years of games and practices.

It's important to set realistic goals for yourself in hockey. Less than one percent of all hockey players turn professional — so the chances of any player becoming an NHL star are very slim. The bottom line is to make sure you're playing because you're having fun.

On these pages you'll find the steps most players encounter on the road that leads to the pros.

STEP 1: Entry level hockey. Most young players begin playing some form of organized hockey at the age of five, six, or seven. The players are often called mites, and the emphasis is on skill development and fun. This level of hockey prepares a player for all the steps that follow.

STEP 2: Squirt. For players under ten.

STEP 3: Pee Wee. For players under twelve.

STEP 4: Bantam. For players under fourteen.

STEP 5: Midget. For players under seventeen.

STEP 6: Junior hockey (Tier 1; Tier 2; A, B, C divisions). For players under nineteen.

STEP 7: College and university hockey.

STEP 8: Professional hockey. Minor pro and the NHL.

How players get drafted

The biggest day of the year for many young amateur stars occurs in June when the NHL holds its annual entry draft. Throughout the season, the pro teams have been scouting amateur players all over the world — in the junior leagues, in college hockey, and throughout Europe. NHL teams also rely on the league's own scouting bureau, Central Scouting, for reliable, current information on star players.

The teams draft in reverse order to the way they finished in the standings in the previous season. For example, in 1984 the Pittsburgh Penguins finished in last place overall and, with the first draft choice, were able to pick Mario Lemieux, who became a superstar.

Although dozens of players are drafted each year, only the top choices are talented enough to step right into major-league hockey.

The majority of the players drafted spend at least a season or two playing for farm teams in the minor leagues.

How important is the annual entry draft? It's all-important. Teams that draft well usually also play well. Teams that misjudge the talent available in the draft and make poor selections are often the same teams that struggle to make the playoffs.

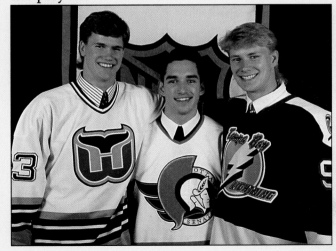

Game day

If you play hockey, you probably get at least a little anxious on the day of a game — every hockey player does. Professional players are no different. Game day is exciting, and it can mean a lot, not only to the team, but to a player's career as well. Let's follow a pro on game day to see what it's really like.

8:00 A.M. I wake up, have a big breakfast, and read the newspapers to catch up on all the news from games played the night before.

9:00 A.M. I leave for the arena. Because it's a game day, our team will be on the ice first, then the visiting team will skate.

9:30 A.M. In the locker room, the team discusses our opponents in the game that night. We talk about who's been hurt and who's been playing well.

10:30 A.M. We're on the ice warming up. It's not like a practice day when we don't have a game. On those days we work really hard, working on our shots, our passes, and line rushes. On game-day practices — or "skates" — we just take shots at our goalies and pass the puck around. We skate just hard enough to sweat, but not so hard that we'll be drained of energy for the game.

11:30 A.M. After practice, I shower and read my fan mail. A couple of reporters and the color commentator from TV are in the dressing room asking questions. I tell them my sore shoulder is okay and how much I enjoy playing with my new linemates.

2:30 P.M. At home again, I have a big pregame meal with lots of carbohydrates for energy, and take a quick pregame nap.

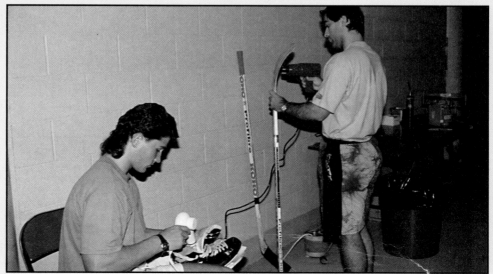

36

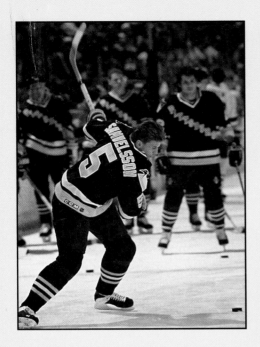

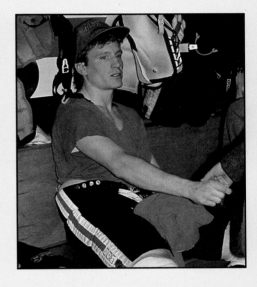

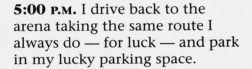

5:00 P.M. I drive back to the arena taking the same route I always do — for luck — and park in my lucky parking space.

5:30 P.M. Back in the dressing room, I check my sticks. I always make sure they are curved and taped just the way I like them. I have my skates sharpened before every game and sometimes between periods too.

6:30 P.M. The coach goes over the strategy for tonight's game — what to look for, power play set-ups, how to kill penalties — and gives us a pep talk.

7:25 P.M. The teams skate onto the ice for the pregame warm-up, which lasts about 20 minutes. The warm-up involves a lot of skating, stretching, and loosening up. The backup goalie stands in the net and handles a lot of shots. When he is warmed up, he gives way to the starting goalie. Often we'll sneak glances at the players on the other team, sizing them up for the game.

7:45 P.M. There's a 15-minute intermission between the warm-up and the game while the Zamboni comes on to resurface the ice. I take care of some last-minute stick taping and check my skate laces. A buzzer goes off to tell us when to get back out onto the ice.

8:05 P.M. After the starting lineups are announced and the national anthem is played, the puck is finally dropped. I feel great in this game and full of energy. I score two goals, which gives me even more energy! The team's really playing well tonight, and we win 4–3.

10:30 P.M. After the game, I'm interviewed on TV because I was selected as one of the three stars of the game. Then I head to the

dressing room to shower. Wow, am I hungry! A bunch of us go out to relax and have our post-game meal. By 1:00 A.M., I'm exhausted and head home to get some sleep for the big practice we've got tomorrow.

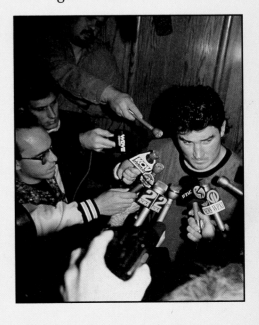

Wear number 13? Not me!

You might say hockey is a sport of superstitions. Once a player gets into a routine or tradition, she sometimes believes changing it will bring bad luck. Superstitious players always take the same route to the arena and hope no black cats cross their paths. In the dressing room, they cringe at the sight of crossed hockey sticks, and they put their uniforms on in a particular way. Often, it's left side first — left skate, left shin pad, left elbow pad and left glove always go on before the right. To do otherwise might bring terrible luck on the ice.

Certain players like to follow the goalie onto the ice, others insist on being the last player out. Before the game begins, it's a "must" for some players to tap the goalie on his pads. As for wearing a jersey with the number 13 on it — forget it. Over the years, only a handful of players have dared to wear that dreaded number. Most feel it could bring instant bad luck.

Hockey players agree it's silly to believe that what they wear to a game or which skate they put on first is going to make a difference in how they play. If they defied tradition and boldly wore number 13, would their legs turn to jelly? Would they suddenly get benched or traded? Of course not, they'll say, but why take a chance?

When **Wayne Gretzky** started playing hockey, he was small for his age and had to tuck his large jersey into his hockey pants. It seemed to bring him good luck so he's been doing it ever since. In fact, he uses Velcro to make sure it stays there.

Phil Esposito always wore a black T-shirt under his uniform.

Star defenseman **Chris Chelios** believes it's bad luck to put on his game jersey until all his teammates have theirs on.

One of hockey's greatest scorers, **Gordie Howe,** wouldn't hesitate to borrow a teammate's stick if he thought there were some "lucky" goals in it.

Colorado goaltender **Patrick Roy** avoids stepping on the lines painted on the ice. Watch him as he carefully steps over the lines while he makes his way to his net. If his skates touch a line he believes his luck will be all bad in that game.

Felix Potvin is another goalie with a good luck ritual. Before each game, this Leaf netminder makes a cross out of tape and sticks it over his dressing room stall.

Former Leaf star **Darryl Sittler** wore his lucky suit and tie before a game one night and scored a record ten points against Boston. He wore the same outfit before a big playoff game with the Philadelphia Flyers and scored five goals in the game — to tie another record. Sittler credits his lucky tie for helping him score the winning goal in overtime against Czechoslovakia in the first Canada Cup series.

Women in hockey

The next time Team USA wins an Olympic hockey championship, don't be surprised if it's a team of women that comes home wearing the gold medals. Women's hockey is growing in popularity — in both amateur and pro leagues.

During the 1993–94 hockey season women made surprising advances in male-dominated pro hockey. Three woman netminders became winning goalies in two pro leagues: Manon Rhéaume and Erin Whitten in the East Coast Hockey League and Kelly Dyer in the Florida Sunshine League. In 1992 Rhéaume had already made history when she became the first woman to sign a professional contract. She became the property of the NHL Tampa Bay Lightning and even played in an exhibition game against the St. Louis Blues.

So women are playing goal in the pro leagues. But why doesn't a woman play center for the Vancouver Canucks? Or defense for the New York Rangers? One reason is the way men and women are built.

Adult men have more muscle and are, on average, larger than women. As a result, men are good at sports where strength and size are a factor. Women have more body fat and tend to be smaller than men, which makes them better at sports that require endurance, such as long-distance swimming or running.

Manon Rhéaume has been playing hockey with boys since she was five, so playing with men in the pro leagues seems natural to her.

This is what women's hockey looked like in 1912. Check out the long skirts, heavy sweaters, and hats. By this time women no longer had to play hockey behind closed doors — they were even allowed spectators.

Abby Hoffman's hockey secret

When Abby Hoffman played hockey with her brothers down at the corner rink, she figured she was just as clever on skates as the boys her age. So in 1955, eight-year-old Abby signed up as a player in a local hockey league as Ab Hoffman, defenseman. And what a player Ab turned out to be! Late in the season, the league selected an All-Star Team and Ab Hoffman was named one of the best defensemen. However, a routine check of Ab's birth certificate revealed something very strange: "he" was listed as a female!

Suddenly, Abby's secret was out, and she became an instant celebrity. Her photo and her story were in all the papers. She was interviewed on radio and television. She received invitations to see NHL games at the Montreal Forum and Maple Leaf Gardens. Nobody tried to bar her from hockey, and she played another year with the boys. Then she decided to give girls' hockey a try. In the girls' league she was outstanding — the most talented young woman on the ice.

Eventually, Abby left hockey and went on to excel in other sports, first swimming, then track and field. In time, she became a world-class runner and competed for Canada in four Olympic Games. But she'll always be remembered as the first girl hockey player to create a sensation by starring in an all-boys' league. Her unique story inspired countless other girls to get involved in hockey.

Canada battled the United States in the final game of the 1994 World Women's Championship. The Canadian goalie was Manon Rhéaume, and the U.S. netminder was Erin Whitten — both play in the pro leagues.

You've just read about some exceptions — and of course men and women can both play all sports. However, it becomes difficult for them to compete together in some sports, such as hockey and football, in which body build and size are factors.

This difference in build between males and females isn't noticeable until about the age of 12, when kids' bodies begin to change. That's why girls under 12 who play on boys' hockey teams are right at home. When the boys develop more muscle, height and weight, girls begin to join all-female leagues.

Some female players look to boys' leagues for their challenge (see page 41). You may have heard about some girls who have taken their cases to court in an effort to be allowed to play along with the boys.

Women wanting to play hockey is nothing new. Organized women's hockey games were being played as long ago as 1890. However, hockey wasn't thought to be really proper for women, so most of the games had to be played behind closed doors and with no men allowed to watch.

During the early 1900s, many women played hockey in college. One team boldly challenged the men's hockey club to a match. But university officials refused to let the game go ahead and even reprimanded the women for their audacity!

You might think the heavy sweaters and long skirts these early-day woman players wore got in the way of playing. Actually, the players often used their long skirts to their advantage, crouching down in front of their goaltenders and allowing their skirts to fan out over the ice. Opposing forwards had great difficulty passing or

During the 1994 world championship the women on Team USA impressed fans with their speed and stickhandling.

shooting the puck through the blanket of skirts.

Women's hockey dropped in popularity during the 1940s and 1950s but picked up again in the 1960s. Major tournaments attracted large numbers of competing teams. By 1987, a women's world tournament was held in Ontario, Canada, and led to an even bigger world tournament — this one supported by the International Ice Hockey Federation — held in 1990. Officials from the International Olympic Committee were so impressed with the caliber of play at these tournaments that women's hockey has been added to the 1998 Olympic games. To help teams prepare for the games, other tournaments have sprung up, including the Pacific Women's Hockey Championship involving Canada, China, Japan, and the United States.

Meet a referee

The fans never applaud them. In fact, they're often booed and called nasty names. But one thing is certain — games wouldn't last very long without them. Referees are as essential to the game as the puck. Here's your chance to meet an NHL referee and find out what his job is really like.

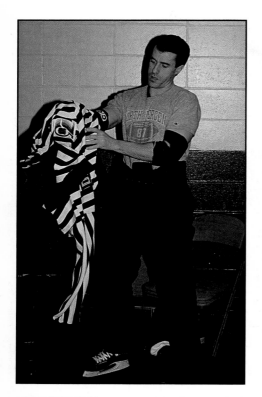

Q. What do you do on the ice?
A. I'm in complete charge of the game. I keep it moving, and when there's a dispute — and hockey always has disputes — my decision is final.

Q. Who are the other officials on the ice with you?
A. They're the linesmen — my assistants. Before a big-league game they check the goal nets for holes in the netting. Then when the game begins, they station themselves close to the boards. Each linesman is responsible for half the rink. Most of their time is spent making offside and icing calls, breaking up fights, and taking all face-offs, except at the start of a period and after a goal. I look after those face-offs. One linesman wears a beeper on his belt, and when the whistle stops play, he often gets a signal from the TV truck. That means it's time for a commercial. After 30 seconds, he gets another signal to tell him the commercial is over and it's time for one of us to face off the puck.

Q. Are there any other officials?
A. There are several off-ice officials at every game — the two goal judges, an official scorer, a penalty timekeeper, a game timekeeper, and a statistician.

Q. What do they do?

A. The goal judge sits directly behind the goal and keeps his eyes constantly on the net. If the puck completely crosses the red goal line, he puts on a red light, meaning it's counted as a goal for the team that put the puck in the net. Sometimes it is ruled "no goal," but that is for me to decide.

The official scorer keeps track of goals and assists. Once the game is over and I sign the official score sheet, no changes regarding credit for goals and assists are permitted.

The statistician keeps track of the players on the ice, counts shots on goal, and compiles many other statistics that are given to the news media. Later he forwards all this information to the NHL office.

Q. What if a player doesn't agree with your decision?

A. If a player gets angry with me and challenges one of my rulings, I may give him a minor penalty, although I will listen to the argument of a team captain or alternate captain. If the player continues to argue, I will give him a misconduct penalty, and if he insists on having the last word instead of going to the penalty box, I will hand him a game misconduct penalty, which means he's out of the game.

Q. How did you learn to be a referee?

A. I started refereeing in minor hockey. One summer I attended a special referees' school to learn more about the business. Then I turned professional and refereed in the minor pro leagues for three seasons. A scout from the NHL — a former referee — liked my work, and the next year I was offered a big-league contract.

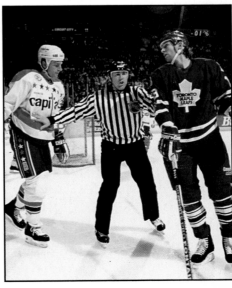

The Stanley Cup

For over 100 years, teams from 17 different leagues have competed for the Stanley Cup. When Canada's governor general, Lord Stanley of Preston, donated the Cup in 1893 to the championship team of Canada, he really started something.

The first team to win the Stanley Cup was the Montreal Amateur Athletic Association. They won a championship series against four other teams to earn Lord Stanley's brand-new trophy, which at that point was called the Dominion Hockey Challenge Cup. What a small trophy it was — a silver bowl about the size of a football and worth about $50.

It wasn't long before hockey teams everywhere in Canada were scrambling after the Cup. Challenges came from places such as Winnipeg, Manitoba; Rat Portage, Ontario; and New Glasgow, Nova Scotia. The most incredible challenge came in

1904 from Dawson City in the Yukon. The Dawson City players traveled 4000 miles by bicycle, dogsled, steamship, and train to challenge the Ottawa Silver Seven for Lord Stanley's trophy. Unfortunately, Dawson City didn't win — in fact, they lost by the largest amount ever in Stanley Cup play. The scores in their two-game series were 9–2 and 23–2. In the second game, Ottawa star Frank McGee scored a record 14 goals.

Today the Stanley Cup is awarded to the best team in the National Hockey League. Teams battle hard to earn this honor, and their fans enjoy every minute of the games.

The final whistle blows, and there is a new Stanley Cup champion! The head of the NHL presents the captain of the winning team with the Cup, then the entire team proudly circles the ice with it. The Cup is passed from player to player until they've all had that chance of a lifetime to carry it. Players, coaches, and managers gather on the ice for a photo, then everyone heads to the dressing room, where the celebrating continues.

Unusual Stanley Cup games

Longest overtime

A game that kept the fans up half the night was played in Montreal in 1936. That night the Montreal Maroons and the Detroit Red Wings staged a tremendous battle through 116 minutes and 30 seconds of overtime before Detroit's Modere "Mud" Bruneteau scored the winning goal in a 1–0 victory. The game was settled in the sixth overtime period — the longest overtime in Stanley Cup history.

Shortest overtime

Some fans were still strolling back to their seats and missed the shortest overtime in Stanley Cup history. When the Calgary Flames faced the Montreal Canadiens in game two of the 1986 finals, the Canadiens' Brian Skrudland scored the winning goal after a mere nine seconds of overtime — a playoff record.

Last-minute officials

Just before a playoff game in 1988 between Boston and New Jersey, the referee and linesmen assigned to the game went on strike. They were angry because a judge in New Jersey ruled that the Devils' Jim Schoenfeld should be allowed to coach his team, even though he'd been suspended by the NHL for remarks he'd made about another ref. So three amateur officials were recruited to handle the game. Only the referee was able to find a striped shirt. The linesmen had to wear yellow practice jerseys, green pants, and borrowed skates. New Jersey won the game, and everyone agreed the substitute officials did a good job.

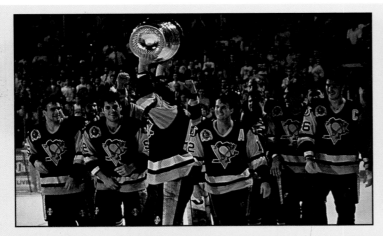

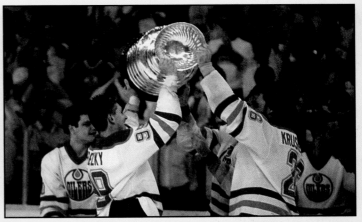

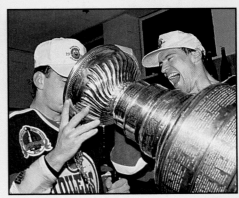

Stanley Cup adventures

If the Stanley Cup could talk, you might find some of the stories it would tell hard to believe. In the past, it's been treated badly, as if no one cared for it. But every year at playoff time, players think of little else but winning it. Chances are no other trophy has been hugged and kissed and photographed more often. Here are some of the Cup's amazing adventures.

The Cup gets the boot

After a Stanley Cup victory party in 1905, the Ottawa champions started homeward. As the players passed the frozen Rideau Canal, one of them dared another to show off his football form and kick the Stanley Cup onto the canal. No sooner dared than done — the Cup was booted onto the canal. The next day, when questions were raised as to the Cup's whereabouts, a couple of the Ottawa players had to hurry back to the canal and retrieve the snow-covered trophy.

The Cup takes a dip

After Pittsburgh won the Cup in 1992, the players were invited to a party at Mario Lemieux's new home. One of the Penguins hoisted the Cup on his shoulder, climbed an embankment overlooking Mario's swimming pool, raised the Cup over his head, and hurled it into the pool. "It's a good thing it hit the water and not the cement bordering the pool," said coach Scotty Bowman, "or that might have been the end of the Stanley Cup!"

All right, who forgot the Cup?

The Cup-winning Montreal Canadiens were on their way to a victory party in 1924 when they had to stop to fix a flat tire. The players piled out to help make repairs. In doing so, they placed the Stanley Cup on the curb. Moments later, spare tire in place, the players took off to the party — without the Cup! When they discovered the trophy was missing, they rushed back to search for it. Sure enough, it was still on the curb, right where they had left it.

Guy Lafleur grabs the Cup

Superstar Guy Lafleur quietly slipped away from a Montreal victory party in 1979 with the Stanley Cup. He stuffed it in the trunk of his car and drove to his parents' home in Thurso, Quebec. He placed it on the front lawn, and people came from great distances to see the famous trophy and have their pictures taken with it. When Guy wasn't watching, his son began filling the Cup with water from the garden hose. Meanwhile, back in Montreal, officials were searching frantically for the missing trophy.

The missing collar

Thieves broke into the Hockey Hall of Fame in Toronto in 1970 and stole the original collar off the Cup. The collar was engraved with the names of early champions. The thieves were never caught, but the collar turned up seven years later in a Toronto parking lot.

CHAPTER 4

Stars of the game

Hockey heroes

Here are some of the hockey legends — some old, some new — who have amazed fans.

Gordie Howe

Gordie Howe is the only player in history to play during five decades. His endurance may never be matched. Howe played professional hockey for 32 seasons from 1947 to 1980 and led the Hartford Whalers in scoring in the 1977–78 season with 96 points — as a 50-year-old grandfather. During his amazing career in two pro leagues he scored 1071 goals. Howe is the only player to play with his own sons in pro hockey (with Hartford in the NHL and with Houston in the WHA), and he's the only player to have his number retired by two NHL teams. The Detroit Red Wings, his original NHL team, retired his famous number 9 in 1972, the year he was inducted into the Hockey Hall of Fame. His Hartford Whalers number 9 was retired on Gordie Howe Night, February 18, 1981.

Ken Dryden

When he was called up from the minors to tend goal for the Montreal Canadiens late in the season of 1971, Ken Dryden became an instant star. He led Montreal to the Stanley Cup that year and became the Most Valuable Player (MVP) of the playoffs. And he didn't stop there — the following year he won the rookie-of-the-year award. Then, before the 1973–74 season, the 26-year-old netminder announced his retirement from hockey. Ken was ready to pursue the career he had studied for at Cornell and McGill Universities — he became a lawyer.

But the Canadiens wanted him back, and he signed with them again the following year, doubling his previous big-league salary. Ken Dryden went on to become the greatest goalie of his time. When he retired for good in 1979, he was a six-time Stanley Cup winner with the Canadiens, he had won the Conn Smythe Trophy, the Calder Trophy, and the Vezina Trophy (five times), and had played with Team Canada several times. He became a member of the Hockey Hall of Fame in 1983, and continues to pass on his passion for the sport through the books he has written and through his continuing enthusiasm for hockey.

Bobby Orr

When 18-year-old Bobby Orr joined the Boston Bruins, they quickly rose to the top of the league standings and won two Stanley Cups. He played for the Bruins in the 1970s, and Boston coach Don Cherry called him the greatest player who ever lived. Orr's chronic knee problems forced him from the game in 1979 at the age of 30. Orr won the Norris Trophy as top defenseman a record eight times in a row and the Art Ross Trophy as the NHL's scoring champion twice. No defenseman had ever won a scoring title before Orr. He also won the Lester Patrick Trophy for outstanding service to hockey.

Wayne Gretzky

For the past fifteen years, Wayne Gretzky has been hockey's brightest star, establishing more individual NHL records than any player in the history of the game. Late in the 1993–94 season, Gretzky became the NHL's all-time leading goal scorer, surpassing legendary right-winger Gordie Howe, who scored 801 career goals in 26 NHL seasons. Gretzky is particularly proud of three single-season records he holds: 50 goals in 39 games, 92 goals, and 215 points. "Those three will be really difficult to break," he says.

After leading the Edmonton Oilers to four Stanley Cups in the 1980s, Gretzky was traded to the Los Angeles Kings in a blockbuster deal. His presence on the Kings' roster created a boom in hockey interest throughout the United States. Gretzky, who is often called hockey's greatest ambassador, was traded to the St. Louis Blues in February 1996. His famous jersey number, 99, is popular wherever hockey is played.

Bobby Hull

His blond good looks and sizzling slap shot earned Bobby Hull the nickname the Golden Jet. Hull was the first NHL player to score more than 50 goals in a season. He and his son Brett (see page 32) are the only father and son to win the NHL's Most Valuable Player award.

Doug Gilmour

In 1993, TV commentator Don Cherry called Toronto Maple Leaf center Doug Gilmour "the best hockey player in the world today." That was after Gilmour led Toronto past Detroit and St. Louis into the Stanley Cup semifinals. Gilmour finished the season with a career high of 127 points and finished second only to Mario Lemieux in voting for the league's MVP award. Instead he won the Selke Trophy, which goes to the top defensive forward in the NHL.

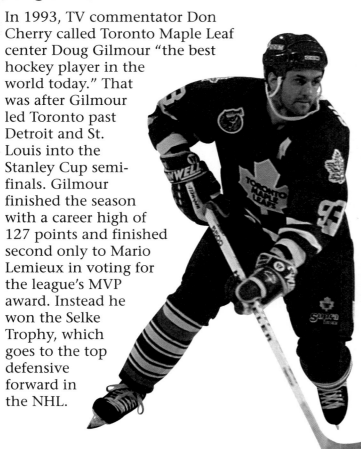

Guy Lafleur

With his fast skating and high scoring, Guy Lafleur led the Montreal Canadiens to four Stanley Cups in the 1970s. This graceful right-winger recorded six consecutive 50-goal seasons and won three scoring titles and two Hart Trophies as the league's MVP.

Mario Lemieux

No player means more to his team than Mario Lemieux does to the Pittsburgh Penguins. Thanks mainly to Mario, the Penguins captured back-to-back Stanley Cups in 1991 and 1992. Lemieux won the award for playoff MVP both times. Other titles he has won include top rookie, scoring leader (he's won this five times), and Most Valuable Player (twice). Unfortunately, health problems have plagued this superstar throughout his brilliant career. His well-known battle with Hodgkin's disease and recurring back problems may force him into early retirement, which would be a huge loss to hockey.

Goal guardians

Billy Smith of the New York Islanders became the first NHL goalie credited with scoring a goal — although he didn't actually shoot the puck into the opponent's net. He happened to be the last player to touch the puck before an opposing player slapped it into his own team's net. But **Ron Hextall** was the first netminder to score a legitimate goal. He scored an empty netter against the Boston Bruins in 1988 and a year later scored a playoff goal against the Washington Capitals, also into an empty net. It'll really be one for the record book when a goalie scores on a guarded net!

It's a wonder **Glenn Hall** lasted as long as he did in the NHL (18 seasons with Detroit, Chicago, and St. Louis). Hall was so nervous he threw up before every game and often between periods. Even so, he set a goalie record that may endure forever by playing in 502 consecutive games.

Behind the mask

It's difficult to believe that when hockey was first played, goaltenders didn't wear face masks! Even though goalie **Clint Benedict** wore a primitive face mask for a game or two in 1929, it wasn't until 30 years later that the goalie mask became a permanent part of hockey.

On November 1, 1959, Montreal Canadiens goalie **Jacques Plante** was struck in the face by a slap shot during a game in New York. After receiving several stitches, Plante returned to the ice wearing a face mask he'd been using in practice. The mask seemed to give Plante new confidence, and the Canadiens embarked on a winning streak. Other goalies followed Plante's smart lead, and within a few years all professional goalies were wearing face masks.

Clint Benedict

Jacques Plante wearing one of his early masks

In 1983, goalie **Tom Barrasso**, 19, moved straight from high-school hockey to the NHL. In his rookie season with the Buffalo Sabres, Barrasso captured the Calder Trophy as top rookie and the Vezina Trophy for being the best goalie — as well as being chosen to the All-Star Team.

Every goalie knows his goalposts are his best friends because they often deflect shots. But Colorado goalie **Patrick Roy** can often be seen talking to his "friends." Roy also has a fast glove hand and incredible reflexes, which have helped him earn the Vezina Trophy three times and the Conn Smythe Trophy as playoff MVP.

In the 1970s, it was trendy for goalies to wear painted face masks. **Gilles Gratton** had a ferocious tiger's head painted on his mask to frighten opposing forwards. **Ed "the Eagle" Belfour** has screaming eagles painted on his mask, while **Gaye Cooley** opted for a goal mask with a happy face painted on it. **Gerry Cheevers** painted marks on his mask to look like the stitches he would have had if the fiberglass hadn't protected him. Today, many goalies have their team crests painted on their masks.

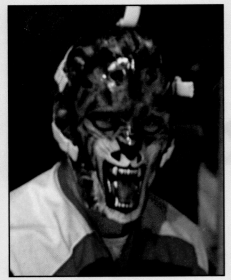

Gilles Gratton

Gerry Cheevers

Ed Belfour

Great moments in hockey

Double play

Toronto Maple Leaf star **Dave Andreychuk** set an unusual record during the 1992–93 NHL season. He became the only player to score 25 or more goals for two teams in one season. Andreychuk tallied 29 goals for the Buffalo Sabres before being traded to Toronto, where he scored another 25 times — for a 54-goal season.

A memorable hat trick

It was the final game of the 1951–52 season, and Chicago was playing the Rangers in New York. The Hawks were trailing in the third period when suddenly a speedy Hawk forward named **Bill Mosienko** caught fire. He scored on rookie goalie **Lorne Anderson** at 6:09, 6:20, and 6:30 — three consecutive goals in 21 seconds. The Hawks won the game 7–6, and Mosienko established a record that has lasted for decades.

Clancy's busy game

Francis "King" Clancy once played every position, including goaltender, in a Stanley Cup game for the Ottawa Senators in 1923. He played right and left defense and took a turn at all three forward positions. Then, when Ottawa goalie **Clint Benedict** was penalized (in those days goalies had to serve their own penalties), he handed his goal stick to Clancy. Clancy took over in goal and held the opposition scoreless until Benedict returned. Clancy was just as versatile off the ice — he went on to be a coach, referee, and hockey executive, too.

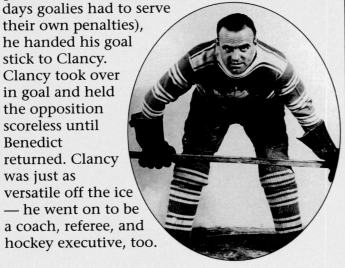

Sittler's big night

On the night of February 7, 1976, at Maple Leaf Gardens, the Toronto Maple Leafs were playing the Boston Bruins. The Leafs' captain, **Darryl Sittler**, was facing a rookie goalie, **Dave Reece**. The young Bruin netminder's big-league career came to an abrupt end after Sittler blitzed him for six goals and four assists in the game. Sittler became the first NHL player to collect ten points in a single NHL match.

A remarkable rookie

During the 1992–93 season, Winnipeg Jets rookie right winger **Teemu Selanne** smashed the NHL record for goals and points by a first-year player. Selanne scored 76 goals and added 56 assists to earn 132 points. He not only passed **Mike Bossy's** previous goal record of 53, set in the 1977–78 season, but also **Peter Stastny's** mark of 109 points, set in 1980–81. Selanne was the unanimous choice for NHL rookie of the year, the first time in League history a freshman player has earned a 100-percent approval rating. In the off-season, Selanne helps with children's causes in his native Finland.

And the winner is...

By now you know the most important team trophy awarded in the NHL is the Stanley Cup, which goes to the winning team after the final game of the playoffs. The Montreal Canadiens have won this trophy a record 24 times.

But there are plenty of other trophies to be won by individual stars, awarded for everything from good sportsmanship to best goaltending. Here's a rundown of some of the most prestigious awards in the NHL.

It's a great honor to win the **Hart Trophy**, awarded annually to the player judged to be most valuable to his team. Wayne Gretzky has won this trophy more often than any other player in the history of the NHL.

The player voted best defenseman in the NHL receives the **Norris Trophy**. In 1993, Chris Chelios of the Chicago Blackhawks won the award for the second time. Chelios is one of only two American-born players to win the trophy. The other is Brian Leetch of the New York Rangers, who captured it in 1992.

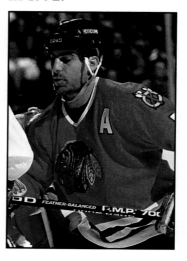

The top goalie in the NHL is rewarded with the **Vezina Trophy**. Former Montreal Canadiens goalie Jacques Plante captured this trophy seven times for the record.

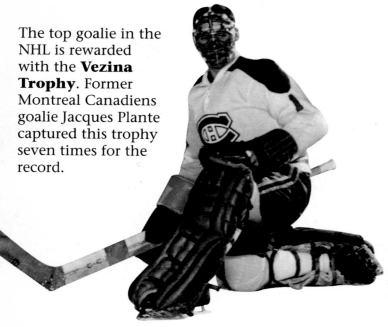

The **Calder Memorial Trophy** goes to the outstanding rookie in the NHL each season. Teemu Selanne is the only player ever to be a unanimous choice for this award (see page 57). Two other incredible Calder winners, Mike Bossy and Joe Nieuwendyk, both scored more than 50 goals in their first NHL seasons.

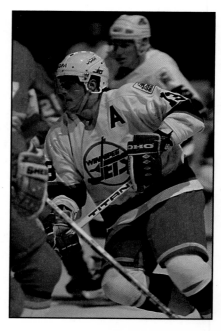

The **Bill Masterton Memorial Trophy** goes to the player who displays qualities of perseverance, sportsmanship, and dedication to hockey. Lanny McDonald is a Masterton winner, and so are Dave Taylor and Mario Lemieux.

The **Frank J. Selke Trophy** is reserved for "the forward who best excels in the defensive aspects of the game." Guy Carbonneau (now with St. Louis) won it three times and was runner-up twice while playing for Montreal.

A season of good, clean play and gentlemanly conduct is recognized with the awarding of the **Lady Byng Memorial Trophy**. Former New York Islander star Mike Bossy won this award three times during his career.

The **Art Ross Trophy** goes to the player who leads the league in scoring at the end of the regular season. Mario Lemieux has captured this award five times and Wayne Gretzky has won it nine times.

The **Conn Smythe Trophy** goes to the most valuable player in the Stanley Cup playoffs. While with Montreal, goalie Patrick Roy became one of the few players to capture it twice — in 1986 and 1993.

The Hockey Hall of Fame

The new Hockey Hall of Fame opened in June 1993. Where else can you test your knowledge of hockey trivia, find out your favorite players' latest stats, relive hockey's greatest moments, and much more? Come on and take a tour.

As you pass through the turnstiles, you're in the Great Moments Zone, with the players, their jerseys, sticks, pucks, and lots of other memorabilia that were important during great moments in hockey.

Now head into the History Zone, where you'll see the first handmade equipment, as well as the heavy wool sweaters players had to wear when hockey was played outside. Did you know hockey teams used to have nine players on the ice, compared to today's six?

In the Marquee Zone you can find out about the arenas where NHL teams play. You'll also see an incredible display of goalie masks. From Jacques Plante's originals to some of the most amazing current designs, they're all here.

Ever been in a real NHL locker room? In the Dressing Room Zone you'll have the chance. Enter this exact replica of the Montreal Canadiens' dressing room at the old Forum, and you can see the players' lockers, find out about the exercise equipment, or even pick up the phone in the coach's office and get a tip to help you play hockey better.

Get ready to get busy in the next zones. You can call the play-by-play of an NHL hockey game, watch a movie, test your hockey trivia know-how, or match your goalie and shooting skills against a computer. You'll also meet some of the real legends of the game, including Maurice Richard, Guy Lafleur, King Clancy, and many more. Don't miss the displays about amateur and pro hockey leagues across North America — add your own team's logo and photo to the database, if you like.

Now you're ready to climb the stairs to the Bell Great Hall. This is where you'll find pictures and information about all the members of the Hockey Hall of Fame. And you'll see hockey's famous trophies. The Vezina, the Hart, the Calder — they're all here, as well as, of course, the Stanley Cup.

Deciding who gets in

How does a player become accepted into the Hockey Hall of Fame? Players are elected by a jury made up of former players, media members, and hockey executives. Three players are inducted each year, and there's also special recognition for game officials, builders of the game, and members of the media. Only a small percentage of all players are inducted, so it's a great honor to be included. For most players, joining the other hockey legends in the Hockey Hall of Fame is even better than the thrill of winning a Stanley Cup.

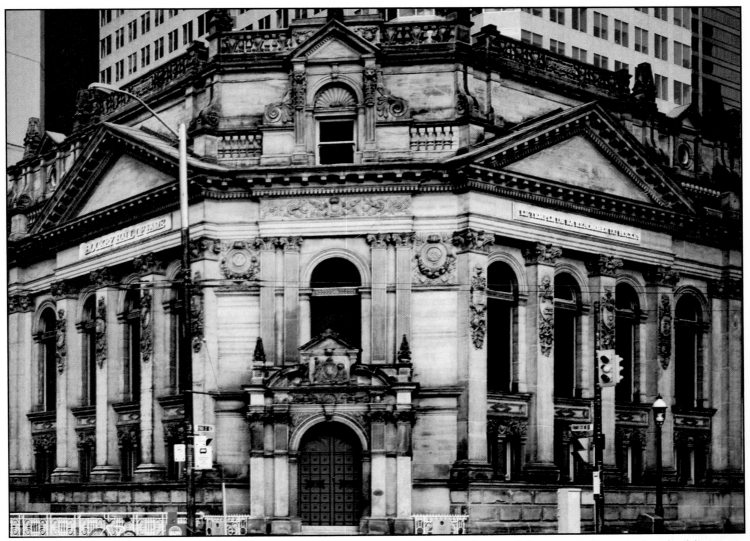

About 500,000 fans visit the Hockey Hall of Fame each year. It's located in the heart of downtown Toronto in a building that's over 100 years old and used to be a bank!

Even Montreal players are amazed at how exact the replica of their dressing room is. The uniforms, the skates, the helmets, — even the hockey tape — are all there.

Make a hockey scrapbook

CHRIS JONES'S HOCKEY SEASON WITH THE **CUBS**

Date	Opponent	Score	Goals	Assists	Points	Comments
10/10	Tigers	4-3 Cubs	0	1	1	Won season opener. I played defense. Coach said I played well.
10/17	Scouts	5-0 Cubs	1	2	3	Had three points but missed my check. Should concentrate more on that.
10/22	Aces	6-5 Aces	0	2	2	Our first loss. Our shooting was bad. I hit the post twice. Coach says forget it, we'll beat them next time.

A scrapbook is great for collecting hockey photographs, clippings and articles, and any other hockey memorabilia you can find that reflects your interest in the game. It's also a good way to keep a record of your own progress as a player. You can keep it forever, and it'll be fun to look back through your scrapbook years from now.

Decide what you want to keep in your scrapbook. You can cut out articles and pictures of your favorite team or player from newspapers and magazines (make sure everyone's read them first). Or keep track of important hockey events that happen throughout the season. Why not write a letter to the team or player you admire most? Most hockey teams are quick to answer their fans.

If you are going to an NHL game, be sure to bring your autograph book. Or, if you know you are going to meet a sports celebrity at a sports banquet or in a shopping mall, get a friend to take your photo with the star. When you tape or paste a photo or clipping in your scrapbook, write a paragraph under it stating why it's included and why you chose to keep it.

If you play hockey, keep a scrapbook about your own life

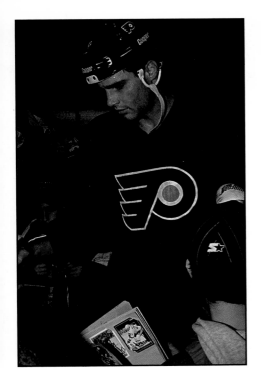

Hockey cards

Did you know hockey cards have been around since 1910 and were first issued in cigarette packs? By 1923 at least four candy companies were distributing sets of hockey cards. These sets are now very difficult to collect — and so are quite valuable — because they were only available in certain areas.

It's important to take care of your cards. A card in mint condition is worth a lot more than one that is bent or torn. So handle your cards as little as possible. Protect them with clear plastic sleeves or binder sheets and store them in a safe place. Don't glue, tape, or write on your cards, and don't bind them together with elastic bands.

Which cards you collect can be important too. Many collectors seek out the rookie cards of players who have the potential to become superstars. The value of the cards can soar if the player becomes a legend.

If you're interested in how much your cards are worth, you can check out their prices in sports card magazines or at card shows. The shows also allow you to meet other collectors and dealers.

What's the most valuable card ever? It's probably Gordie Howe's rookie card. It was issued in 1946 and is worth $3500 in top condition!

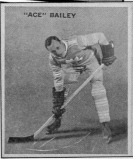

and adventures. You can keep a game-by-game account of your season. Set it up like the example on page 62 and include scores of games, personal goals, and assists, as well as your own summary of the games played. At the end of the schedule, write your account of the season in your scrapbook, and don't forget to include any team pictures and crests you received.

Index

Anderson, Lorne, 56
Andreychuk, Dave, 56
assists, 45

Barrasso, Tom, 55
Belfour, Ed, 55
Benedict, Clint, 54, 57
blue lines, 5
Bondra, Peter, 20
Bossy, Mike, 57, 58, 59
Bowman, Scotty, 48
breakaway, 16
Bruneteau, Modere "Mud," 47

Calder Memorial Trophy, 51, 55, 58, 60
Carbonneau, Guy, 59
changing lines on the fly, 7
checking, 6–7, 16, 28–29
Cheevers, Gerry, 55
Chelios, Chris, 39, 58
Cherry, Don, 51, 53
Clancy, Francis "King," 57, 60
coaches, 6, 28
Cooley, Gaye, 55

defensemen, 5, 6–7
defensive play, 4, 6–7
defensive zones, 5
drafting, 35
Dryden, Ken, 51
Dyer, Kelly, 40

equipment, 18–19, 20–21, 26–27
Esposito, Phil, 38

face masks, 54–55
face-off circles, 5
farm teams, 16, 35
Fedorov, Sergei, 20
forwards, 5, 6
freezing the puck, 17

game day, 36–37
Gilmour, Doug, 53
goal lines, 5
goaltenders, 5, 6–7, 51, 54–55
Gratton, Gilles, 55
Gretzky, Wayne, 26, 27, 38, 52, 58, 59

Hall, Glenn, 54
Hart Trophy, 53, 58, 60
hat tricks, 16, 56

head-manning the puck, 17
Hextall, Ron, 54
Hill, "Chummy," 11
history of hockey, 8–9
hockey cards, 63
Hockey Hall of Fame, 49, 60–61
Hoffman, Abby, 41
Howe, Gordie, 39, 50, 52, 63
Hull, Bobby, 52
Hull, Brett, 26, 32–33, 52

ice. See rinks
icing the puck, 14

Kariya, Paul, 20

Lady Byng Memorial Trophy, 59
Lafleur, Guy, 49, 53, 60
Leetch, Brian, 58
Lemieux, Mario, 27, 35, 48, 53, 59
levels of hockey, 34–35
linesmen, 44, 47
Lord Stanley. See Stanley, Baron of Preston

McDonald, Lanny, 59
McGee, Frank, 46
McGill rules, 9
masks, 54–55
Masterton Memorial Trophy, 59
Mosienko, Bill, 56

neutral zone, 5
Nieuwendyk, Joe, 58
Nilan, Chris, 13
Norris Trophy, 51, 58

offensive play, 4
offensive zones, 5
officials, 44–45
offsides, 15
Olympic hockey, 40, 43
Orr, Bobby, 51
overtime, 5, 47

Patrick, Joe, 18
Patrick Trophy, 51
penalties, 12–13, 45
periods, 5
Plante, Jacques, 54, 58, 60
playing shorthanded, 12, 14, 17
point man, 17
positions, 5–7
Potvin, Felix, 39

pucks, 10–11

ragging the puck, 17
red line, 5
Reece, Dave, 57
referees, 44–45, 47
Rhéaume, Manon, 40, 42
Richard, Maurice, 60
rinks, 4–5
Roenick, Jeremy, 26
Ross Trophy, 51, 59
Roy, Patrick, 39, 55, 59

Schoenfeld, Jim, 47
scoring, 30–33, 45
Selanne, Teemu, 57, 58
Selke Trophy, 53, 59
shutout, 17
Sittler, Darryl, 39, 57
skates, 8–9, 18, 20–21
skating, 22–25, 28
Skrudland, Brian, 47
Smith, Billy, 54
Smythe Trophy, 51, 55, 59
splitting the defense, 16
Stanley, Baron of Preston, 9, 46
Stanley Cup, 9, 46–49, 58, 60
Stastny, Peter, 57
stickhandling, 6, 25, 28
sticks, 9, 19, 26–27, 37
superstitions, 38–39

taping sticks, 27, 37
Taylor, Dave, 59
Taylor, Fred, 25
teams, 5–6
trophies. See specific trophies

Vezina Trophy, 51, 55, 58, 60

warm-up exercises, 22–23, 37
Whitten, Erin, 40, 42
women's hockey, 40–43

zones, 5